An Elmore County Life

An Elmore County Life

Daniel H. Thomas

NewSouth Books
Montgomery

NewSouth Books
105 S. Court Street
Montgomery, AL 36104

Copyright © 2003, 2016 by NewSouth, Inc.
All rights reserved under International and Pan-American Copyright Conventions. The text of this book was first serialized in 1992 in the Eclectic *Observer*, Eclectic, Alabama, then published with permission of the *Observer* in book form by the Black Belt Communications Group (now NewSouth, Inc.). Historical photographs were provided by the City of Wetumpka and the Elmore County Historical Society and Museum. A special thank you for photographic research to Joe Turner and, for the earlier editions, Elizabeth Speer Gillian, of the Elmore County Historical Society and Museum. Thomas family photographs were provided by the author. The ISBN of the 1992 edition was 1-881320-01-4. The 2003 edition was published in the United States by NewSouth Books, a division of NewSouth, Inc., Montgomery, Alabama, with the ISBN 1-58838-059-9 (LCCN 2002152806)

Publisher's Cataloging-in-Publication data

Thomas, Daniel H.
An Elmore County life / Daniel H. Thomas.
p. cm.

ISBN 978-1-60306-024-0 (paperback)
ISBN 978-1-60306-425-5 (ebook)

1. Thomas, Daniel H.—Childhood and youth. 2. Wetumpka Region (Ala.)—Biography. 3. Wetumpka Region (Ala.)—History. 4. Wetumpka Region (Ala.)—Social life and customs—20th century. 5. City and town life—Alabama—Wetumpka Region. 6. Thomas family. 7. McCoy family. I. Title.
F334.W48 T48 2002
976.1'52—dc21

2016938533

Printed in the United States of America

Fourth Edition

Contents

    Foreword / 7

1   Roots / 15

2   Early Memories / 24

3   School Days / 32

4   High School / 38

5   Focus on a Career / 42

6   Remembering Father / 46

7   Tragedy Strikes / 50

8   Sports and Girls Discovered / 56

9   A Young School Teacher / 61

10   Conclusion / 68

Foreword

MARINELLE STOWE

In the spring of 1989, Dr. Daniel H. Thomas, a distinguished Elmore County native, wrote his memoirs for publication by the *Eclectic Observer*. His is a warm, readable account of early days in Wetumpka. Upon reading it a few older citizens may do some reminiscing of their own and younger readers will learn much about how things "used to be."

When Margaret Elizabeth Thomas came with her young sons to Wetumpka in the 1880s she probably knew little of the historical significance of this area. The McCoy family, on the other hand, having lived in Alabama longer, may have been more familiar with the town on the banks of the Coosa river and other nearby historical sites. Neither family could have foreseen the contributions a grandson would later make toward preserving that history.

At first there were two towns—East Wetumpka and West Wetumpka—with business houses on both sides of the river. In 1839 the two towns were incorporated as one. Being at the head of river navigation Wetumpka soon became the center of commerce for much of Alabama as well as parts of Tennessee and Georgia. Big double-decker steamers were putting in here several times a week to load and unload cargo and passengers.

The naturalist William Bartram visited the area in 1777, and a New York newspaper later declared that Wetumpka, with Chicago, was one of the two most promising towns in the West. In the 1840s, Wetumpka had missed becoming the capital of the State of Alabama by only one vote. After sixteen ballots in the Legislature, however, state records were transferred from Tuscaloosa to Montgomery.

But by the time the Thomases and McCoys settled here, the town had begun to decline. Railroads were replacing river transportation. Devastating fires in 1844 and 1852 had demolished whole blocks of the business section east of the river. On the west side most of the brick stores had been torn down and the bricks moved to Montgomery to build stores there. (It is said that the bricks for the hotel later owned by Mrs. Thomas came from an old hotel on the west side of the river.) Floods in 1833 and 1844 had done much damage to both residential and business sections of the city. A later flood in 1886 was to destroy the picturesque covered bridge built in 1844. The war in the 1860s and subsequent economic problems also took their toll. Wetumpka's population dropped from 5,000 to around 500 in just a few years.

However, the history of this area goes back much further than the founding of the town of Wetumpka. Just a mile from the Riverside Inn, the hotel owned by Mrs. Thomas, and almost within sight of the home of Daniel and Mary Elizabeth McCoy, is the site of the Indian village commonly called Hickory Ground. An important Muskogee town, it was here that the Scotch trader Lachlan McGillivray found and married Sehoy, a princess of the ruling Tribe of the Wind. Lachlan and Sehoy (according to historian Albert Pickett) were the parents of Alexander McGillivray, who was chief of the Muskogee Creeks for many years and who was called by Pickett "the ablest man ever to set foot on

Alabama's soil." At one time he held commissions in the armies of the English, French and Spanish while he negotiated treaties on behalf of the Indians. McGillivray maintained a residence at Hickory Ground, though his permanent home was at Little Talise near present-day Wallsboro.

About three miles south of Hickory Ground, at the junction of the Coosa and Tallapoosa rivers, a large mound is evidence of a prehistoric Indian culture. The mound is thought to have been ceremonial; ancient burial urns have been found nearby.

Near the mound, the French established Fort Toulouse in 1717, as both a military and a political outpost. Because of its strategic location at the head of a great river system and in the midst of numerous Indian villages, it was extremely important to the French and served for many years as a deterrent to British expansion and as a means of keeping the local Indians neutral in the on-going rivalry for control of what is now the southeastern United States. Trade with the Indians flourished—animal skins for guns and other European-made goods.

After his victory at Horseshoe Bend during the War of 1812, General Andrew Jackson established a fort, later named Fort Jackson, on the site of old Fort Toulouse. Though the town never materialized to any significant extent, it is remembered today by a road leading to it from Montgomery known as the Jackson Ferry Road.

The Indian leader, William Weatherford, called Red Eagle, came here to make his peace with Jackson, and the Treaty of 1814 was signed here; that treaty surrendered half the heartlands of the Upper Creeks and opened much new territory for white settlement.

This is the area where Dr. Daniel H. Thomas, scholar, historian and author, grew up. Here he went to school, listened to tales of the old timers, and walked along the river banks where artifacts of the Indian cultures could still be found. Old Fort Toulouse held a special fascination for him.

It is not surprising that when he later attended the University of Alabama he chose Fort Toulouse as the topic for his master's thesis.

In the years that followed Thomas specialized in modern European diplomatic history, researched and published articles and books, received a Ph.D. from the University of Pennsylvania and eventually became chairman of the history department at the University of Rhode Island. He never forgot his interest in French Colonial history, however, and in the late 1950s began rewriting his thesis of thirty years earlier.

The Fort Toulouse Memorial Association had been formed for the purpose of gaining national recognition of Fort Toulouse as well as preserving the site. Under the direction of Mr. William M. Thomas (no relation to Dan), this group raised money to pay French students to research old French records under the supervision of Dr. Thomas, who took sabbaticals to go to France and England for this purpose.

Materials from books and papers written during the thirty years since the original thesis were also researched.

The resulting revised and expanded manuscript comprised the entire Fall 1960 issue of the Alabama Historical Quarterly published by the Alabama State Department of Archives and History. It was reprinted in 1989 in book form as *Fort Toulouse: The French Outpost at the Alabamas on the Coosa*. The introduction was written by Dr. Gregory A. Waselkov, assistant professor of anthropology at the University of South Alabama.

It is interesting that archaeological excavations begun in 1972 clarify and supplement the conclusions of Dr. Thomas.

As a result of the efforts of Mr. W. M. Thomas and other members of the Fort Toulouse Memorial Association, supported by Dr. Thomas's findings, Fort Toulouse was dedicated in 1961 as a National Historic Site. Federal and state funds have become available, and with the assistance of Alabama Historical Commission members and Friends of the Fort, the Elmore County Historical Society and others, the area has been developed and now is an educational, historical and recreational park enjoyed by thousands from all over the county.

For Dan Thomas a dream has come true. Fort Toulouse finally has its rightful place in history.

The late Marinelle Stowe was president of the Elmore County Historical Society.

An Elmore County Life

Walter E. Thomas was a deacon in Wetumpka's First Presbyterian Church, built in 1857.

1

Roots

It is now customary for memoirs to begin with one's "roots," the failing memories of what one's family traditions or family Bible gave as its origins. In my case this will be a description of the Margaret Elizabeth Thomas family coming from Abbeville, South Carolina, and the Daniel W. McCoys from Fredonia in Chambers County, Alabama, to the more promising town of Wetumpka on the banks of the Coosa, a more promising land. Both families had farming backgrounds; they did not desert farming altogether, but their principal interest here was business.

My future Grandmother Thomas had a husband, John Harris, but she wore the britches and was soon known as "Old Miss." My grandfather-to-be McCoy had a wife, Mary Elizabeth, who was content to run her household, while he tried to run Elmore County and then various businesses in town.

Giving first attention to the Thomases, Old Miss had sufficient capital in June 1896 to buy a large 50-55 room three-story brick hotel she renamed the Riverside Inn, since it overlooked the Coosa. She quickly made it a popular, important, and profitable institution for a small town.

But to go back to deeper roots, both families were Scotch-Irish;

that is, their ancestors were originally Scotch who had emigrated to Northern Ireland where they took on some Irish characteristics but remained Protestant. Then the potato famine of the middle decades of the nineteenth century had driven them like thousands of others to the southern United States. Like so many Scotch-Irish, they crossed the Appalachian Mountains, then turned south down one of the beautiful valleys.

My families' choice of Wetumpka was at the end of one ridge: the Tallapoosa drains its eastern slope and the Coosa the western. Their junction is a few miles below Wetumpka where the French of Louisiana constructed Fort Toulouse in 1717, and Andrew Jackson had to reconstruct a fort in the War of 1812 which his superiors named Fort Jackson. If you stand in the middle of the bridge in Wetumpka and look to the east, there are rolling hills. Upstream, there are rapids. To the west and down-river the land is as flat as your hand, and tile depth permits navigation the 150 miles (300 by river) to Mobile and the Gulf.

Upon the acquisition of the hotel, fortune smiled on the Thomas family for a time. In those days a good hotel in a county

The Riverside Inn

seat was a far more significant institution than today. The Riverside Inn adjoined the business section, and a couple of hundred yards of brick sidewalk led to the bridge; more importantly it was even closer to the Elmore County courthouse. This was, of course, the local government center and the location for frequent court sessions which meant sizeable attendance by lawyers and judges (local and circuit) and witnesses, not to mention onlookers who wanted to attend sensational trials.

These folks could book reasonable rooms at the hotel and enjoy the dishes prepared in the famous Old Miss Thomas's kitchen. Traveling salesmen, called "drummers," would rent rooms to display their wares for sale to merchants. There was a spur rail line of seven miles from Wetumpka to the main line of the L.&N.R.R. at Elmore, and a horse-drawn hack carried passengers to and from the depot on the west side of the river. There probably was hack service also to a suburb of Montgomery where street cars ran into the city.

Strangely enough there were relatively fewer stores on the west side of the river and nothing like as many homes on the east. Yet strong rivalry in sports existed between the two sides of town, the business side's playing field a short distance down Main Street being called something like "Bougaloosa." I would guess that the population was about 850.

Another practice unusual to our present generation was that young married couples, who had as yet no houses and were not well-to-do, could afford room and board at the hotel, as could widows and bachelors. A few of the well-known couples who did so were the Will Cousins and Will Laceys (Senior), and so would my future parents. But I am getting ahead of myself.

I do not know just when the Thomases arrived in Wetumpka, but it was in the 1880s. I doubt that my father, Walter E. Thomas, the eldest of three sons, stayed in school

A political rally in Wetumpka in the late 1800s or early 1900s.

more than five years. Even when a young man my father, not six feet tall but appearing more than that to me, was fat but exceptionally agile for his weight, which rose to 270 pounds. When I was ten or eleven I challenged him to a foot race, but I never made that mistake again.

Clean-shaven, he had a full head of black, wavy hair and relatively firm features. He was quite mature for his age, since he opened his own butcher shop when still in his teens. It was just across from the hotel and he soon added groceries. Later in these memoirs, when I was old enough to work in the market-grocery store (I have often said I was reared in this store, a half-truth) I will tell of the tribulations of running a market in those days. But I will now say Daddy had to have cattle and hogs to butcher, and these had to be bought on scouting trips around the county to locate farmers who had them to sell, or to raise them himself. He did both. Then they usually needed fattening so he rented pastures on which they could graze and rented land on which to cut hay and raise many bushels of corn, oats, and velvet beans to feed them.

Needing a place in town where cattle and hogs could be fattened and butchered and a place to store corn, oats, beans and hay, he purchased a cotton warehouse about a block away. It is now owned by the city, is in good condition, and is called the Alliance Warehouse [and now houses the museum].

In his farming Daddy habitually looked to the county agents of Auburn for the best scientific ways to farm. Convinced that farmers should not rely so heavily on cultivating cotton, he only cultivated a small field, smilingly calling it "your mother's cotton."

Of course an entrepreneur needs customers, and being very gregarious by nature and having unlimited energy, my father joined not one but three fraternal societies or lodges which he attended regularly: Masonic, K.P., and Odd Fellows. He enjoyed playing dominos and cards with his cronies. He was a civic-minded person and very soon after he came of age he was elected alderman of the city council and he held that position until his untimely death at age thirty-nine. Later in these memoirs, I will relate some of the municipal improvements which he promoted. He once told Mother that he could make money in the middle of the desert, and I believe he could. He was, as you will agree, what today we would call "a take-charge guy."

One early and lesser way he displayed this talent, one I could judge very early in life, was that by acclamation he became Elmore County's premier barbecuer. This was evident when in 1912 the monument on the site of Fort Toulouse was unveiled by the Alabama Society of the Colonial Dames of America before a large attendance including a boatload of big-wigs from Montgomery. Preparations began the day before under Daddy's instruction when a long trench was dug, fires were set, and cooking of quarters of meat began. Or he might prepare a small barbecue for two to three dozen at Valley Brook on some holiday. I recall a much smaller occasion, when Uncle Claude Thomas was a visitor from Selma, and a dozen men had a barbecue up on a hill beside a brook in which some beer bottles were cooled for an unusual libation. Need I add that it was for the men only?

By his mid-twenties Daddy was ready to marry, build a home, and have children. The girl for whom he set his cap was a recent high school graduate, Lucy Carlton McCoy, daughter of Dan and Mary Elizabeth McCoy, who lived a long mile down the Old Montgomery Highway. The census of 1860 shows that Dan McCoy's father (D. H. McCoy) had a large plantation up in Chambers County; he was a Baptist who preached on Sunday and kept abreast of national and sectional affairs. He was a great admirer of the distinguished Daniel Webster (Secretary of State and Senator) who, although he abhorred slavery and was against its extension, opposed its abolition because he predicted that would cause the South to secede and a horribly bloody civil war would surely result. So my great-grandfather had named his next son, born in 1852, Daniel Webster McCoy, but being inclined toward politics the latter always preferred to be called Dan. (I am indebted to one of my best-remembered students, Frank D. Jones of LaFayette in Chambers County, for information on my great-grandfather.)

When the predicted Civil War began, the planter raised a company and led it to war. In time young Dan moved to the Ware community several miles north and northeast of Wetumpka about the same time the Thomases arrived. When elected sheriff, he moved to Wetumpka. He chose a place on the edge of town and land on which to do some farming, although political office (election next as tax collector in 1900) and business were his chief interests. Once I teased him by saying, "Grandpa, they say you deserted the Democratic Party." "I did not!" he exclaimed. I countered by asking, "But didn't you later run as a Popolite?" "Yes," he admitted, "but the Democrats deserted *us*." Some of his business ventures included a laundry which burned within two weeks and was not yet insured, a cotton gin which succeeded, and an ice house which failed, the latter through no fault of his own. A large Montgomery corporation, which had tried to buy him out, simply sent wagon-loads of ice to Wetumpka and left a piece at the back door of each house until my granddaddy had to close. The "Trust," as townspeople called the monopolistic corporation, then doubled the *former* price of ice.

After her family moved to the outskirts of Wetumpka, Lucy McCoy began to have a rather lonesome childhood. Her older sister, Willie Mae, married Joe Sanford Clifton in 1898; her sister, Ruth, who would become Mrs. Talmage Sanford, was years younger. Living in the country, a mile from Wetumpka and across the river from school, she could ride with her father in the buggy, but he left so early that she would have a long wait in the streets of Wetumpka, so she generally walked alone to school. Once there, one particular teacher was "difficult," but my future mother did well in other studies.

As Walter Thomas pushed his suit for marriage, young Lucy McCoy held out for a time. Her ambition was to become a lawyer! Later she would say to me, "Son, there's a very interesting case being tried next door in the courthouse. Why not go over and observe what's going on? I think you would find it interesting." I did go, but lawyering was not for me. I think she would have enjoyed a career as a lawyer and would have been a good member of the bar. But a young small-town girl studying law in 1903? As usual, my father got his way. They were married in the First Baptist Church on January 7, 1904.

It was a dazzling event and was widely attended, as reported by the *Herald*. To mention only one decoration, the "ropes of green, thickly dotted with white roses, reached from the four corners of the church to the central 'chandelier.'" The music was by an orchestra. Old Miss also out-did herself in the glittering reception in several rooms of the hotel; she too had an orchestra. Aunt Daisey Thomas's slice of the wedding cake contained a thimble, a sign of early marriage, and she did marry later. The groom's piece contained a dime—surely not a prediction but a confirmation of his prosperity. The young couple lived in the hotel pending the construction of a home.

At once Mother became Daddy's help-mate: she worked in the grocery store which was connected with the butcher shop by a large arch. Soon she became the manager, kept the books of both businesses, and was named manager of the Wetumpka branch of the Western Union Telegraph Company.

The thorough Walter Thomas also carefully chose just the proper location for his home. He purchased several acres on East Bridge Street up the hill over-looking the center of Wetumpka. It was only five minutes away, going downhill, but longer uphill since that street was so steep that in some places steps must be used. To go by carriage or car there was a circuitous street. He needed the several acres because, besides a house, he needed a "lot" for the livestock and in time three barns, two buggies, two horses, a cow, wagons, mules, corn cribs, a hack room, stalls, and a branch to supply fresh water for the livestock. Also he needed space for a large orchard for peaches and pears. I do not recall any apples but we sold them in the store.

I do recall with the greatest satisfaction the fig trees. No insects preferred these, and I made a lot of money selling quarts of them which were in great demand by housewives since no other preserves tasted half as good. The big problem was to pick ripe figs before the birds got to them. I would not have minded this so much if these competitors had satisfied their appetite by eating the whole figs, but they insisted on taking a peck or two and then moving on to another ripe fig. Unlike the birds, Wetumpka housewives never had a sufficiency.

Of course Daddy had to have a vegetable garden, which even had a row of raspberries and some pomegranates. There was room for a small house for the farm hand's family and the cook. The house he planned and began to construct at once had large rooms with high ceilings because of the hot climate, a wide front and side porch and a back porch.

2

Early Memories

My parents were financially able to afford some expensive features in their home. For example, each room except the three very small ones had a beautiful large mantle piece, a "William Morris" no less. Each had a tall round column on the sides, with a large mirror above and attractive tiles the width of the mantle piece.

The house my father first planned and began to construct was sufficient to house Mother, Daddy, and me—I was expected by the end of 1904—and perhaps a sister. But misfortune then struck the Thomases for whom things had been going so well.

On a Sunday afternoon in October 1904, after presiding over the noon dinner in the hotel, Grandmother was alone except for her young grandson to whom she was reading. He was Thomas Harris Williams, an orphan. He would become the well-known "Tubby" Williams, who would marry Jessie Moody of Wetumpka, have a successful career as a high school and college coach, and with Jessie would establish the Williams School in Montgomery. An improperly banked fire in the kitchen—a separate, wooden structure—must have spilled coals and started a fire that spread to the hotel proper.

Many of the townspeople who might have fought the fire via a bucket brigade, since there was no fire department or water system, were across the river at the cemetery where a prominent citizen was being buried. Did Grandmother grab a double-barrelled shot gun and fire two shots, the customary signal for a fire and a call for help? I don't know. But it was a large brick structure with a slate roof, and a sufficient number of people did arrive to save a few valuables and pieces of furniture. Someone threw Mother's jewel box out a window to Granddaddy McCoy who did not notice that her wedding ring fell out. It was found by an on-looker who kept it for years. Then a quarrel with a neighbor occurred and the finder was forced to return it to Mother.

But the entire hotel structure and most contents were lost. I thank Eugenia Law for one of her many articles in the *Wetumpka Herald* based on interviews with my mother and an article in the *Herald* on the fire.

At least Grandmother had insurance on the hotel amounting to $6,000, about one-fourth its value. Also lost was a barn with 800 bushels of corn—which must have belonged to my future father—and the insurance for that amounted to $500. But since the hotel had a slate roof, my father's market-grocery just across the street from the hotel and other neighboring structures were saved. Fortunately our families were close-knit and, pending the completion of the new home, my parents were taken in by my beloved Aunt Willie Mae and Uncle Joe Clifton and their daughter Mary Dean. This was on The Hill only a couple of hundred yards to the north.

Since it's an ill wind which blows no good, the tragic fire contributed to the city council's decision to establish a municipal water system and a volunteer fire department. Water was piped to almost the entire area of the municipality, but the equipment was quite primitive. A fire bell capable of a piercing and rapid staccato (and to me hair-raising) clang was placed on the roof of a downtown building. It could be rung by two chains or ropes reaching down to the sidewalk below. When the volunteers responded, they headed for a two-wheeled cart with regulation fabric hose wound around its center. It could be pulled to the appropriate fire plug by any available buggy or wagon and later by auto. But the members did have firemen's hats and coats, and a nozzle for the captain. And who was elected the first captain on the department and thus would direct the nozzle? My own Dad!

Another effect of the fire was that Grandmother Thomas and her unmarried children and Thomas Williams now had no home. So my father (note that I didn't say my mother) was persuaded to enlarge the plans for the house so it would be sufficiently large to include her family. A wide hall divided the house down the middle: Grandmother's family would live on the east side, Mother and Dad's on the west, and the extra front room on the east was a joint parlor. There were, however, separate kitchens and dining rooms.

In the meantime I was born on December 6, 1904. (When I was sufficiently old to enjoy presents, this was too close to Christmas to please me.) A few months later my family moved the short distance from the Cliftons to our half of the new house.

When we moved into our new home in 1905, the two households made it a busy place. There were my mother, father, and me with my sister Margaret Elizabeth arriving five years later. Grandmother had her young grandson, Thomas Williams, a single daughter who was Aunt Daisey (most delightful and with whom I was very close), and Uncle Claude (a handsome pharmacist educated at Vanderbilt).

Although my mother was a working mother, I had these close relatives who could help keep an eye on me. Also on our side of the hall we had a black cook and housekeeper who also looked after me. The first one I recall was Janie Mann whom I adored; when for example she would take me downtown on a Saturday afternoon, I would fight off any man who pretended to make passes at her.

The cook arrived early and we had a big breakfast of hot cereal, meat, eggs, grits, biscuits, and milk or coffee for adults. On Sundays the meat was salted herring which came to the store in small wooden kegs. The dinner was always at noon, and we had biscuits for the meats and corn bread for the vegetables. The cook left in mid-afternoon, and it was generally understood in those days that cooks could take some food home, as long as they left enough for the mothers to warm up for supper.

Until age five I had serious health problems: typhoid fever, a swallow of iodine which I thought was tasty cough medicine when playing doctor, and a scalding by hot water a cook threw out of a high kitchen window. The latter did not scar me, however. Our bulldog went mad and bit me, so I was taken to Atlanta to the only Pasteur Institute in the South, for the twenty-one daily injections. Then I had double pneumonia. When recovery was long-delayed the diagnosis was at first tuberculosis, thus hardly curable. But Surgeon L. L. Hill of Montgomery gave the second and correct opinion—empiema (puss on my lung).

Dr. Hill cut out a part of a rib in order to clean out the infection. Thereupon, he reminded me that God had created woman out of Adam's rib and announced that he was going to repeat the miracle: he would use mine to create a sister for me. Sure enough my redheaded sister Margaret Elizabeth Thomas was born a few weeks later. The family tradition has it that by that time I had caused my father to be $5,000 in debt. Perhaps so since I have not listed such simple operations as removal of tonsils and adenoids.

Sister's arrival was a most happy event. She was a healthy, bright, and beautiful baby. Grandmother persuaded our family to enter her in a baby beauty contest held on the west lawn of the old county courthouse. I do remember that her baby carriage had only what the family called simple sunflower decorations, yet she won. Somehow, when Eugenia (Edwards) Law's older brother commented on the win, I resented it and attacked. He brushed this off, and I was not too clear over it myself, because I wasn't ashamed about her award.

I recall that when she was only three years old, she had what I think was her only visit by a doctor in her childhood. She fell off our large dog and cut her forehead, so the doctor sewed it up without anaesthesia. Her screams led me to run beyond ear shot. Within several years, the scar receded into her hair. When five, and she had to wear eyeglasses, I walked outside and broke into tears.

She shared her mother's care and attention to grooming, as for example the time we were hurrying to school and she fell and tore a hole in her ribbed stockings. (I was used to those stockings, because boys in those days also had to wear them, since we wore knickers until about age thirteen.) She insisted on returning home for another stocking. I nicknamed her "Priss" and she never objected to it.

I have vivid, early memories of the phobia I had about fires which all seemed to occur at night. Roofs were usually wooden shingles and thus fires were horribly visible from our house high on The Hill. When that frightening rapid clang of the fire bell woke us up and Daddy donned his fire coat and hat and raced out, Mother and I were at the window. Once when we could see no blaze, she noticed that I turned blue with fright, fearing it was our house.

When I was eight or ten the biggest blaze we ever saw appeared

Walter E. and Lucy McCoy Thomas, with Dan in 1909 in Atlanta where he was receiving injections for rabies.

to be our store, so I persuaded Mother to allow me to run down The Hill to make sure. It turned out to be the beautiful three-story DeBardeleben house which had been constructed on the site of the hotel. The wind blew southward toward a large cotton warehouse. Although my father received some criticism, he decided that it could not be saved, so he first directed the nozzle so as to wet down the facade of his store and then try to save what bales of cotton could be salvaged. Saving a five-hundred-pound bale of cotton that has once caught fire is tricky: when the fire appears to be extinguished, it may suddenly flare up again. So a few bales were even rolled down into the river for a day. I recall with pride a kind of initiation rite to advanced boyhood if not early manhood: after a fire I helped the volunteer firemen drag the hose to a grade in a street so the hose could be well drained before rolling it back on the cart.

Fire was a serious threat to life and property in early Wetumpka. The building in the background here was the Fifth District Agricultural School, completed in September 1897, and destroyed by fire in January 1906. The young men in this 1905 photo made up Wetumpka's first football team; Gordon Robison was captain.

3

School Days

I was so pleased with Wetumpka's Fifth District Agricultural School (F.D.A.S.). Note that it did not bear the name "High School."
In those days the federal government permitted each congressional district to have one school based on the same concept as Auburn; that is, a school which had an experimental farm so students could apply theory studied in class, and l am told that at one time graduates could enter Alabama Polytechnic Institute as juniors. The early football teams even played Auburn, and in one game the school held Auburn to six points.

There had been competition among municipalities to acquire a congressional district school, and Wetumpka had succeeded. Completed in 1906, it was an impressive, modern, three story building. It had a most beautifully appointed auditorium, seating five hundred, a stage with electric footlights, a school library, *and an indoor gymnasium.*

The latter was in the basement and two huge, round steel pillars were on the court itself, but most communities the size of Wetumpka had no indoor basketball court or large auditorium. Today of course every high school has an indoor gymnasium, but too often there is no large attractive auditorium in which all or most of the students could attend instructive assemblies and join townspeople in evening events.

I am so glad, for example, that I could hear perhaps our greatest rival to Daniel Webster for the title of America's leading orator, William Jennings Bryan. He was quite hoarse when he began, but the real timbre of his voice soon came through even if I could not long remember his message.

By the time I entered F.D.A.S., the agricultural aspects were passing. By the time we reached high school, my classmates were not interested in farming, but I did see small plots on the campus on which each girl in some class ahead of me could raise a tiny vegetable garden, and there still was a so-called experimental farm.

When I entered school in 1911, we had both the first and second grades in one room. I do not recall much about these grades except that the teacher enforced discipline with a large ruler which she applied to the palm of the miscreant.

We moved to a room across the hall for grades three and four of which I have a better memory. One day I approached my teacher and asked if I could move away from the "Drones Row" of desks for students who would not study.

This was a row directly against the left wall and its aisle was wider than the others. She replied logically that I had sat there

During the building of the Fifth District Agricultural School.

for some months and asked why I wanted to move. I confessed that I "have just learned what a drone is." She wisely explained that I would have to show for at least a week that I no longer deserved a place on the row I found degrading.

I began to study as a busy bee should. And I alerted Willie Ben Robinson, who had a desk across the wide aisle, to expect me to hand over my books and papers at the exact same time the next week, provided of course that the teacher herself had not moved me off that row. She hadn't. So when she turned her attention to the other grade, Willie Ben and I made the exchange.

I have always appreciated that teacher's concept of pedagogy since it worked in my case. I am greatly indebted to her, though I can no longer recall her name. I continued to study and by the fifth grade was a fair student.

I realize that in recent decades this teacher's concept is passé, but I think this has been carried to such extremes that it is one explanation for the current dissatisfaction with results of our teaching in public schools.

In my teaching years, I have thought that students who did not or could not do well in the usual courses should have, after a

Female students gardening at the Fifth District Agricultural School.

year or two, a chance to attend other schools or other courses in their school where they could develop natural skills and trades.

If they felt such a transfer was a stigma, they could try harder to avoid them; if not, I believe they might in time take pride in acquiring skills and would be happier there. In recent decades those who acquire skills in such trades can usually earn a good living.

Another event in that room which was memorable was a set-to with a long-time schoolmate, Jesse Pollard Johnson. In warm weather boys nagged parents until they let us go barefooted. Jesse Pollard was always heavy, so he had sufficient dead skin on the side of his toe through which he now stuck a pin. In the space between the back of my desk and the seat, he stuck his toe containing the pin into my back-side.

Having moved from the Drones Row, I was busy at work; being annoyed and with the teacher giving her attention to the other grade, I wheeled around and cracked him over the head with a pencil so hard I broke it. (It was a paper pencil.) Then I rashly dared him to meet me after school for a thrashing. He did both. As usual in my fights, I was thrown, my opponent sat on me, then he pinned down my arms and laughed at me.

Suddenly we heard a voice: it was the school principal. Thinking we were going to be punished for fighting, we quickly claimed we were only playing. But he reminded us of his repeated rule that every student must go directly home after school and then, if parents permitted, we could be on our own. He ordered us to appear separately in his office the next day for a paddling. Each of us obeyed. The principal picked up a wooden paddle, ordered me to bend over a chair, and paddled away.

I do not remember whether it hurt at that time. That was of no consequence, because in that one grade, my father had promised me the large sum of five dollars if I received no paddling. After the school year, Daddy picked the worst possible time to ask if he owed me five dollars. He was sitting at the head of the dinner table, and his presiding was impressive, especially when we had company as we had at that meal. With a hang-dog expression, I had to acknowledge that I hadn't earned the reward. His laugh was as loud and clear as my spirit was low—and that's when that paddling hurt.

Two grades in one room is not as bad as people now conclude. At least these students had several study periods daily—or at least a chance to study. And that is more than present-day public school students usually study at home, where the noise-level is probably higher than it would be in a two-grade room.

Jesse Pollard's sister was another teacher I admired. She was Mary Lockette Johnson who later became Mrs. William B. Thomas and the mother of William M. Thomas of Montgomery. He and I are not related, but we have long shared a common interest in local history.

Unlike most of the boys, by the third or fourth grade there was one girl I adored—at least at a distance. In the fifth grade, that length was shortened to an aisle: on the day school opened, I arrived early, which was most unusual for me since I was a dawdler. (I now realize how much this habit annoyed my father.)

I milled around until she (Lela Leslie Bailey) chose her desk for the year. Quickly I picked mine—just across the aisle. That was the year I gave her candy as a birthday present—not Nunnalys, but one of the small glass thirty-five-cent jars stocked by our store. Later she became such a beauty that she was one of a half-dozen campus queens pictured in the class book of '25 at the University of Alabama. You can judge that royalty was far above my league.

The seventh grade was a big hurdle. Before I reached it, the county had given the tough requirement of a county-wide exam for entrance into high school. But the F.D.A.S. still had Miss Fielder as its seventh grade teacher who was feared for her standards and discipline, so she gave excellent preparation for high school. And all of her attention could be given to one grade.

Our class of some forty-two students in the seventh grade was reduced to twenty-nine freshmen admitted to high school, although of course some who were held back made it on their second try.

My domestic duty in these days which I recall most clearly was to bring in two scuttles of coal and some kindling each cold evening and build the morning fires for my parents and sister.

4

High School

The W. B. Thomas Butcher and Green Grocer was the name of my parents' store. By the time I had become familiar with the store, I recall our excitement of having telephones. Our numbers were so early that they were low: the store was ten and the family phone was 3J.

The butcher shops in recent decades have changed much more than grocery stores. Not only did small town butchers have to slaughter the animals, their days began before daylight. A meat cutter had to hitch our beloved John to a small wagon, drive to the shop, cut up meat, place it on a cloth, cover it, and drive up and down residential streets so housewives could pick their meats for breakfast and noon dinner. Our driver could walk ahead of John and whistle for him to keep up.

The shop would open early. Hamburger and sausage meats had to be cut up by hand, then ground by a loud engine, and the quarters of meat had to be sawn and sliced by hand and made ready for sale or to be cut to order. Huge blocks of ice had to be raised by a pulley and shoved into the top of the refrigerator every several days.

The day would not end until someone at the Gamble

Hardware would strike two tempered steel plows together at six o'clock. Although loud, this was a welcome indication that it was time to close, but on weekdays only.

On Saturdays it was customary for country people to pour into town. Streets were crowded with wagons, buggies, and, later, autos. Sidewalks were so densely packed that I often stepped off to make my way through town.

A very few of the rural people who could not afford a noon meal at a hotel or restaurant would come into our grocery store for a lunch. When clerking in our store, I could serve it. The preparation and fare were simple.

A piece of paper was spread on the counter, a can of stewed tomatoes was opened and placed on it with a spoon, and a bottle of pepper sauce. Next I cut a small slice of cheese from the large wheel which had a blade attached and a gadget which could measure the size of the portions. I followed with a handful of crackers and presto—a meal for fifteen cents which would suffice until back home, and no tip.

On Saturdays we remained open until eleven p.m. at least, and then, in the market, we had to scrape the blocks thoroughly, clean the whole market carefully, get rid of the sawdust on the floor, and spread a fresh batch. If the market had taken in seventy-five dollars it was a good Saturday, and half the cash flow of the week. The take by the grocery was less than half that. Yet the market required a full-time meat cutter in addition to Daddy who worked part-time, and one or two others to help on Saturdays

Just before going home close to midnight, I would be sent to Little Sam's Cafe with a T-bone steak and an onion for each one of us, and the chef would broil these on top of his stove. Back in the store we would have a small feast and call it a week.

We did deliver several orders each day by a bicycle which had no gears. When old enough I became the delivery boy

The horse-drawn delivery wagon of the "old reliable" Thomas Market.

on Saturdays and in summers. The packages were placed in a wooden box which rested on the handlebars and frame, a very cumbersome arrangement but good for developing legs: only in late years did I realize it was hard on the cartilage of my knees.

Since Mother managed the Western Union business at her desk, she did receive income for this service but she or someone also had to work for Western Union on Sunday mornings.

When I asked Daddy to teach me how to cut meat, he refused, explaining that he didn't want me to be a meat cutter. He did not know then how much that skill would pay when it was unionized. As for unions, Mother was required to belong to one. During the years when Western Union business was good, the company paid her a wage; but when business was slack, she received a percentage of the income, whichever was less.

It was in this period when I decided on a career. Our new school principal in 1911 was Dr. A. S. Ford. Puzzled by his title since he wasn't a physician, I learned what a Ph.D. was. That's when, hopefully, I chose the profession of college teacher. When Florida McBride replaced ailing Janie Mann as chief cook and dishwasher and her husband became my father's new hand, she gave me the nickname of "Doctor" long before I earned any degree.

5

Focus on a Career

As has been said about most people, I think many of my characteristics had been shaped by my twelfth year. Mother undoubtedly had the most influence. It is true that she was a working mother all her life, but I never felt neglected. It's true also that while others went home after school, I went to the store; if she was not there I could find her at Miss Molly Doster's millinery shop.

Mother was always carefully coiffured and groomed, and ornate hats were an important feature of a woman's clothing. She was a tall and very erect person, and Sister and I inherited these characteristics. She possessed the kindest, most expressive gray with tinge-of-blue eyes. Her very silk-like brown hair eventually turned gray but never white; it was not wavy, but frequent visits to the hairdresser took care of that.

She had such an innate sense of psychology that it was very easy to accept her views and guidance. I recall the time, when I was about five, that she heard me use some four-letter, old English words. When asked where I had heard these, I replied, "at the cotton warehouse down The Hill." (Today's children do not know what fun we had racing wildly along the top of rows of five-hundred-pound bales of cotton, knowing that if you fell their softness kept you from getting hurt and you could not damage the cotton.) Gently and without reproach or commands, she explained that some people did use such words; but they were not used in polite society, so it would be better never to do so. Since that day I have detested their needless use.

One time I threw a small piece of bread in the fireplace. She quietly explained that it was a sin to waste food when some unfortunate people didn't have enough. I never thought to ask if she meant this as a sin in a religious context, or that it was a shame to do so. I took it to mean also not be wasteful. When Sister began to sing and I made fun of her voice, Mother asked me why. I replied that we both knew Sister couldn't carry a tune in a bucket. True, Mother said, but did I enjoy making her feel bad? I really didn't, and that conversation helped Sister and me to get along remarkably well. If I shouldn't make fun of my sister, I shouldn't make fun of anyone.

Like most kids, I began to smoke corn silks and grape vine stems. Soon I asked Mother what she would do if she caught me smoking. "Nothing," she replied; she hoped I wouldn't smoke until I was eighteen, but if I was determined to do so, that we sold tobacco, and I could have all I wanted. The only thing she asked was that I do so openly, before teachers and the public, because she wanted no son of hers to sneak "behind the barn." So help me, my next smoke was when I was a college freshman; it didn't taste much better, and I never developed the habit.

I was strongly influenced by other pieces of her advice. If ever I started a fight, or hit someone without cause—the first to strike—I should be punished; but if I was struck first by someone, and I didn't get in the last blow, I ought to be punished for that. I took that advice, too, the only trouble being that when in pickup games, I had a way of judging that someone had in effect roughed me unfairly, so I would come out slugging.

Slugging is too strong: we were too young to do much harm and didn't aim at the face, so my opponent usually threw me, pinned my arms down, and laughed at me. But that didn't stop me from swinging away the very next time I felt wronged. Schoolboys and young men fought so much more often in those days than they do now.

Once Mom told me that I might be challenged by a black boy (we said "colored" in those days) for no reason except a challenge. She asked me simply to make no reply, just ignore it. Sure enough I soon had one from a boy I knew quite well and who was no larger than I. We had no quarrel, but only a block from home he challenged me by saying he could whip me. It was hard, but I half smiled, kept walking, and our cordial relations remained the same.

Another advice had strong influence on me: "If poverty comes into a home, love is apt to fly out the window," Mother believed, so she advised me not to marry until I owned a home. I did not enter that state until age thirty-five, although one reason for that late date was the Depression.

Both parents taught and maintained high moral values. Mother was a Baptist and Daddy an Elder in the Presbyterian Church, so I attended the latter and became a staunch Calvinist. The Sunday School teachers and the ministers taught the Ten Commandments and such great respect for the Sabbath that when my busy parents decided to take some recreation such as a movie which was not available to them except on Sunday, I refused. However, when I got hungry—I usually was, Sabbath or not—I could spend my money on ice cream, even though the soda jerker was working on Sunday. I soon grew up, however.

At first I took Sister to Sunday School. But she became bored after the superintendent, saintly Louis Cantelou, led us through the opening exercises, and we divided into separate classes. If she fretted and cried a little, the superintendent would quiet her by taking her out for a walk until Sunday School was over. This was fun for her but embarrassing to me, so I laid down the law: if she cried one more time, I wouldn't take her! She did, and I refused, so Auntie Ruth McCoy carried her to the Baptist Sunday School, and she later became a good Baptist.

My Sunday School teachers such as Miss Mary and Miss Eula Cantelou hoped I'd be a minister, but I realized I was not the type to preach; I liked history and was fairly good at telling "his-story," but not philosophy or theology, and so I never even taught a Sunday School class. I did give some thought to becoming a foreign missionary, but soon returned wholeheartedly to the ambition of teaching.

School teachers influenced me of course, but that was more by examples than precept.

Naturally my father also influenced me. When quite young the most interesting part of the day for me, when my father was home, was the three of us sitting on the front porch in the cool of the evening with me in his lap and we talked as he smoked his after-supper cigar. I kept after him to let me smoke it until finally he said that if he did, I would not draw on it. When I assured him to the contrary he finally handed me the wet, well-chewed cigar. I got a good taste and some smoke. It was so awful that I didn't try another cigar until a banquet at the University of Alabama's initiation into an honor society. Since cigars were at each plate, I tried one, but didn't like it either.

6

Remembering Father

I have happy memories of incidents such as the time I had that pneumonia and Daddy, knowing I was terribly thirsty, took out the knife he always carried in his pocket, scraped an apple with a blade, and fed me the cool, delicious, essence of the apple. Nothing ever tasted better.

He was capable of a quick, immense temper. I recall two occasions in which he came close to corporal punishment. Once was when I refused at first to let Auntie Ruth instead of Mother dress me for Sunday School. The other was when he thought I had kept on fishing after he had sent for me. He had begun to cut a sizeable branch for that purpose, and that gave me a chance to explain that I had not received his message. At least I never had to lock horns with him.

I took after my father in many more ways than in stature and height. I recall what a great pleasure I had when he would take me along as he drove in a buggy to check how a crop was doing, and we would see who could come closer to guessing the number of cars we would see. Later, when I was almost twelve, he raised me into Seventh Heaven when he said he thought it was about time "to buy your mother an automobile."

"What make?" I inquired, and ascended still higher when he asked if I agreed it should be a Dodge, my favorite make—or was it a Reo? He did not live sufficiently long to make that purchase.

As Grandmother Thomas had less and less influence in my life, my grandparent McCoys played a greater and exceptionally happy role. When I was two or three, it was agreed that I was old enough to spend the night with them. I was happy about that until two-thirty a.m. when I woke up, did not find my parents, and screamed for them.

Always patient with me, if not with everybody, Grandpa hitched up his buggy and drove me a mile up The Hill. But soon I realized that having these grandparents living in the country was great. Grandmother McCoy spoiled me and Auntie Ruth, their daughter, was great fun.

Among her accomplishments was that Talmadge Sanford (senior) dated her on Sunday, Wednesday, and Friday nights. Like other gentlemen of that day, he kept his sweetheart in two- to five-pound boxes of candy, Nunnallys of course, and I was rationed by my aunt to two pieces a day. Almost as enjoyable was the way she could pound out my favorite on her piano, "Oh, You Great Big Beautiful Doll." Also when they had dates I could sit with her and her beau for at least twenty minutes a night.

She frequently had me ride with her in the buggy, until one day (in 1910) as she drove into the middle of Wetumpka, I heard her exclaim: "Lord, there's Papa in an automobile!" I bounded over the wheel, rushed up The Hill, packed a small bag of clothes, and lived for a time at Grandparent McCoys if not in the back of that beautiful car. In those days the purchaser of all cars except Model Ts could have a chauffeur for a couple of weeks to teach someone to drive. The local girls were always wondering who the chauffeur really was, and if he was polished in his manners, he was suspected of being the Black Sheep of some wealthy family.

(I am reminded of a trick that two mischievous boys would play on a driver. Each would light an old-fashioned lantern and wait until a car drove into sight with gas "headlights" on, these being little brighter than lanterns. The pair would hold hands and trot toward the oncoming car; when close, they would each turn and trot to the side of the road.)

There were other reasons for good times at the McCoys, such as when farmers in the neighborhood pitched some hay in a wagon, and drove some of us kids to the Alabama State Fair. At the race track I was lifted to a shoulder so I would thereafter be able to say: "I have seen Dan Patch, the World's Champion Trotter." Almost as memorable was a demonstration of a wheel which the inventor, a Montgomerian, claimed would prevent trains from derailing.

He hoped that railways would install them and he would make a fortune. At least in the demonstration I saw, a locomotive was driven along a track which had a sledge hammer lying across the rails, and it was not derailed. In time Auntie Ruth taught me to drive, for in those days drivers' licenses were not required.

In my twelfth year, my father began to introduce me to his farming as well as business interests. One Saturday in the fall of 1916 he included me among his cotton pickers of a small crop, getting me out about daybreak. I was delighted and was sure I would make him proud of me by picking as much as one hundred-fifty pounds of cotton, three-fourths as much as regular pickers. But by nine a.m. my back ached, and I lowered my estimate by half.

In April 1917, when World War I was in its third year and we were about to enter, corn and cattle prices were going up rapidly. So he rented three fields to cultivate. But he had decided on a big increase of acreage in corn by renting an unusually large field of "bottom land"—I think this was his first such venture.

It was tempting because of its potentially high yield; yet it *was* so close to the Tallapoosa River it might be flooded if we had far more than usual rain that summer. But he decided to chance it. He took me there one day when he supervised the work of several hands. To boost morale and because Daddy himself liked a good time mixed with hard work, he decided that we should go "muddying" in a nearby creek. It was my only such experience. He picked out a sizeable pool in the creek, and the several of us jumped in and began to stir up the mud so that the fish would come up for air and we could toss them up on the bank. It was a good take. When we thought the mission accomplished, the fish were evenly divided—a pile for each participant.

In mid-afternoon he had his youngest hand go with me to throw two fishing lines in the river. We did catch a four-pound catfish, my first and most successful fishing in this manner.

7

Tragedy Strikes

The crop proved to be the most promising ever. But then two of the greatest tragedies of our family occurred simultaneously. In August 1917, heavy rains occurred. Of course the rivers rose. That alone would not have seriously threatened the very large corn field. But the Alabama Power Company had decided to generate more electricity by increasing the height of the Tallassee Dam up the Tallapoosa and had used timbers to do so. These proved to be too weak. The pressure of the rising water forced the timbers to give way. The most beautiful and bounteous of all of Dad's fields was quickly inundated. Not an ear of corn was saved.

Far worse than that, Daddy had become ill. The first diagnosis was indigestion, but the actual cause was appendicitis. So he was rushed to the L.L. Hill Hospital in Montgomery. That proved to be too late: Daddy's appendix burst and peritonitis set in. It was fatal. He died an agonizing death on August 5, 1917, only thirty-nine years old.

My father was far ahead of his time in the conviction that corn, oats, beans, cattle, and pastures were much more appropriate and profitable for Elmore County than cotton. I am thinking also of the many municipal services which he supported during the fifteen or so years he was on the city council: the water and the fire departments, stone sidewalks in the residential area as well as business, the municipal electric power plant, and garbage collection. Yet he was a practical person, as when he was the one selected to find and purchase a mule to be used in the collection of garbage.

But one of my father's hopes had not been realized. He knew that Wetumpka had once been a thriving river port, but only a few steamboats still anchored there. Perhaps this means of low-cost transportation could be somewhat revived. It was known that if only two or possibly three dams with locks were constructed in and above Wetumpka, boats could steam over the rapids and have navigable water all the way to Rome, Georgia. This would mean some 315 miles—as the crow flies—to the Gulf.

Of course federal appropriations would be required for the construction. As a youngster my father had witnessed what appeared to be a good start: an appropriation was available to construct one pair of locks just below the bridge in Wetumpka, but not sufficient for a dam, also. Yet this was half a loaf. Thomas Irving, a young English engineer in the construction of the locks, courted and married Daddy's sister, Jessie Emily Thomas, in 1895. (The young couple later moved to the small town of Seattle, Washington, where he was the town engineer and had much to do with laying out the streets of downtown Seattle, now considered one of the most attractive cities in the whole world.)

It was after this that Walter Thomas bought the large warehouse and the land down to the river at the very spot where ships then anchored. A.E. Thompson has painted an interesting picture of a loaded steamboat which was moored there in the late 1800s. The hotel clearly appears between two pine trees in the picture. One of the buildings appearing above the steamboat may *possibly* be the warehouse which my father purchased. The covered bridge and the rapids under and above the bridge are clearly visible.

For years my father was active in an organization, the Coosa-Alabama River Improvement Association, which promoted the idea of constructing the dams and locks essential for the Rome, Georgia., to the Gulf waterway. Am I wrong that it would have been one of the longest navigable streams, if not the longest, in the whole eastern half of the United States? Instead of thinking this was just a pipe dream, take a good look at a map and see if you agree with me that this plan would have been far less expensive and a far more practical project than the Tennessee-Tombigbee (Tenn-Tom) river and canal system.

And would not this route to the Gulf have been in a more populated and industrial area than the Tenn-Tom? By the way, my friend Billy Thomas tells me that The Coosa-Alabama River Improvement Association still exists. Now its principal purpose is to protect the water flow of these and nearby rivers.

From the "vision thing" to the petty-personal: I inherited my father's razor, strop, mug, brush, and soap and saved them until time to use. Of more importance was a beautiful gold watch, a large Waltham his mother gave him when he was eighteen for not using profanity.

There lingers in my mind bits of a song my father loved to sing. It was about an old fellow "who washed his face in a frying pan." I don't think it was entitled "Old Dan Tucker," a song old-timers often refer to, but I have been unable to confirm the correct title or learn the words. Can any reader do these for me?

As a diversion to help overcome my genuine trauma due to Daddy's death, I was promoted to long trousers and given a trip to Selma to visit Uncle Claude. He was becoming the principal figure in the very successful Tillman Drug Company, and I have often wondered why many more businesses didn't follow his practice of having all full-time employees become the stock holders of the business—a successful profit-sharing plan.

My father appeared in my dreams for the next sixty years.

Poor mother. She was, of course, devastated by the death of my father, the loss of a small fortune by the flood, and all the responsibility now resting on her shoulders alone. She was, however, a strong if quiet-spoken person.

She did break down at times. Once when she did, she did not notice a stranger who stepped just inside the grocery store, noted her sobbing, backed out, went across the street, and reported what he had seen. He learned why, and he would in time play a major role in her life.

He was Edwin J. McCowen, a Texan who had just arrived in town with a carload of mules to sell to Elmore County farmers.

She was left with a daughter of seven and a son soon to be twelve. Sister Margaret developed into a student who won highest school and college honors, and became a college instructor, only to develop nephritis when still in her early twenties. This could not be treated successfully at that time. But at least we found the best research professor and physician of that disease who enabled her to live an almost-full life, to marry Professor William Wright Kirk and to live free of pain until she was forty.

She died when only a year older than her father when he passed away. My brilliant, lovable sister and one of the best pals I ever had! I have a happy memory of a long weekend in which I traveled to a Cleveland hospital to visit her and noted how several of her nurses stopped to chat, after their tours of duty, as much to be cheered up by her as to be of good cheer.

Thanks to her full knowledge of my father's finances and business affairs, I found in Mother's papers the figures she tallied up soon after the funeral. She knew to the dollar the debts which he owed and which were owed to him and if they were collectable. I am amazed at her list of the quantity of livestock, corn, oats, wagons, and other pieces of equipment used for the store and for farming which he had collected. From her figures I learned that my father had achieved his success without going into huge debt. His life insurance, which was moderate, was twice his debts. With justified pride Mother never had to spend my father's insurance. She had a superior business head herself.

She employed a Mr. Whitaker to close out the farming side of my father's activities, and Mr. Robert Hallonquest to manage the market. The latter, a long-time and close friend, would also relieve Mother from some of the long hours required by Western Union business which was conducted over the telephone. Like other business people, Mother would have many problems in the post-war recession in the South.

Among her still later positions Mother was secretary for such men as Stephen B. Reneau, tax collector, H. M. Lewis, the county agricultural agent, the agent for the Farm Bureau Insurance Company, and realtor W. E. Strickland. The position she liked best was as a warden at the Julia Tutwiler Prison for Women where she treated any inmate with respect as long as she deserved it.

Meanwhile, Grandmother Thomas and her family one by one moved from her apartment up on The Hill.

So Mother asked if the Cliftons would occupy that part of the house. Uncle Joe and his family were willing and it was a very happy arrangement for us. I was so very fond of Aunt Wille May and Uncle Joe (naming my new puppy after him), Mary Dean (a few years older but who was a good playmate even so), and a sister, Willie, younger than I but a playmate for a longer time and to this day a very close first cousin. There were simply no other boys near my age on The Hill, so I enjoyed the privilege of being the teacher or principal when playing school, our major "sport," with these cousins and a few neighbors our age. Uncle Joe had succeeded Daddy as fire chief and he was constable and the entire Wetumpka police force.

But tragedy struck again and soon: Uncle Joe Sanford Clifton developed an abscess and died several months later (April 1918). In a short time both grandmothers and Aunt Daisey also passed away.

As was the custom of the time, in all these cases, including my father and sister, the casket lay in the parlor or living room where a portion of the burial service was held. About the same time attorney Frank W. Lull, a popular mayor, and the successful editor, Howard Rose Golson of the Wetumpka *Herald*, our closest neighbor, also died. You can imagine the sad influence these deaths had on remaining members of our family.

I became well acquainted with the Grim Reaper. Decades later, in addition to my only sister, I was to lose my first wife, Margaret Mawhinney Thomas, in 1972, just after her sixty-first birthday, and my second wife, Marjorie Taggard Thomas, in 1990.

As you read these memoirs you can judge that my teaching career would be a happy experience. But my personal life did not maintain that level of good fortune. Cousin Willie Clifton, a good observer who has such wide personal experience in this feeling, insists that "worry never kills anyone," and I agree.

But I was fortunate enough to have my mother until her ninety-seventh year (1980).

8

Sports and Girls Discovered

Of course in high school we had different teachers for each subject for the four year program of that time. I recall that Mr. Hughes and Miss Smiley, who now lives in Montgomery, were among our favorite teachers. I was flattered to be elected president of the class, but some of the girls deserted me for a newcomer my junior year.

I did study but was not a really good student: Inez Collins, Lela Leslie Bailey, and Margaret Tate were among the several who were superior in our senior class of sixteen. I must say that I do not think we had a sufficient number of good courses in writing and literature. Such courses would have been a great aid to me. There was no city or county library, and my reading was embarrassingly thin—such as all of the Tom Swifts, some Tarzans and not many others.

With the ambition for graduate degrees and college teaching, you can imagine how much reading I would have to do in later life. I wish I had been required to write numerous papers. But I am grateful that the objective type of tests and exams (such as true and false) had apparently not been discovered. I regret that they ever were, and I never used them when I taught.

Joe and Luke Sewell were the best-known athletes but they were two or three years ahead of my class. Their brother, Tommy, was a classmate. They drove in an open Ford all the way from Titus.

But athletics had to take a back seat by my senior year. There was no money for a faculty-coach, but Tubby Williams, then in business, was an excellent volunteer coach of football, sometimes assisted by Phil Enslen, both formerly Marion Institute players. Every single piece of the uniforms for our thirteen players was scruffy hand-me-downs or had to be purchased by the player, and only one did so.

Like others I had little or no padding in my gear, not even shoulder pads. I was sixteen and weighed one hundred-thirty-seven pounds fully dressed. I did make the team and started four games. But a latecomer who bragged in my presence that he would find a way to get someone's place on the team thrust his knee into my left kidney three days later. I could not run for three weeks and lost my place as a starter. Unable to even imagine a teammate would do such a thing, it took me years to realize that his injury was intentional.

To my surprise we won the first games with Clanton and Prattville, lost 50-0 to Sidney Lanier, and won about half of the games if I recall correctly. William Tandy Daniel, Watt W. Jones Jr., Jesse Pollard Johnson and B. Gorman Jordan were some of my friends on the team as was John Lewis Edmond (Buddy) Collier, our best back. Other good friends of mine who did not go out for athletics were Fletcher Sedberry, who attended the Starke School in Montgomery, and Charles Parker Sedberry, still a special friend of mine.

I also played basketball, which Tubby coached. Although by that time I was the tallest on the squad, I was as poor in that sport as in football. I have always claimed that my feet were too big (size 12-D even then) for me to be a good athlete. I played center on the small squad. I should explain that the usual age for entering the first grade had been six. But since my birthday (December 6) was close to September, I had been permitted to enroll at age five. Thus I was the baby of my class—at first physically and always socially. So I doubt that the permission of early enrollment was good for me.

Readers will notice that I have not mentioned any organized recreation. There was none.

Occasionally Mr. Stephen B. Reneau would pass the word around to boys that we should have a Boy Scout Troop. This was excitingly agreeable, but we never became actual Scouts. He would arrange for us to camp out or to use a friendly farmer's barn near some place we could swim, such as Harrigate Springs or the Speigner Lake, and we would have a hilarious time for one night. One of our quieter, simple pleasures was walking up the hills to the east of town. On Sunday afternoons several would gather on The Hill and follow the long, slightly-used paths to the highest point called Bald Knob. Today there may be houses on it, but I am not sure—if so, I did not recognize it.

A family would sometimes arrange for a party, as when Sara Cabot Robinson (Pierce) had a memorable Easter egg hunt. Later my Mom agreed, and for several years we had New Year's Eve party. There were refreshments, and each boy and girl had cards similar to old-time dance cards, and we would sign up for five-minute "dates." Then each couple would take a walk, timed by a clock. Some couples may have held hands, but I did not see any. It was dark outside, so it was OK to take your date's arm.

We were always free to gather around the piano or Victrola in Rev. Moseley's home for an evening. Churches had annual hayrides to a safe place up the river or to the beach at Speigner Lake for a swim and picnic lunch each had brought. Many of us had no bathing suits and went in with pieces of our regular clothes.

When older, two or three boys would decide to sponsor a dance. They would get the Clifton Hotel to agree to a dance in its dining room, collect four or five dollars from boys, and hire a three-piece orchestra to play until eleven p.m. We would have such a good time that some boy would go around and collect perhaps a dollar so as to have the orchestra play thirty minutes longer. Stags were welcomed by both sexes.

We had no Little League or Pee Wee-age leagues. As a matter of fact, the National Recreation Association did not favor such youngsters being organized into leagues with schedules and uniforms.

In my junior year Mother asked me to stop by the Western Union office on the way to school. When I did she told me she was planning to get married. This was a tremendous surprise, but it shouldn't have been. She was only thirty-five, and Daddy had died three years before. Also, the groom-to-be was Edwin J. McCowen, the Texan who had found her crying and had backed out of the store three years earlier.

He had remained in Wetumpka, had sold my mother cows and hogs for the market, had become a partner in the business, and "Mr. Mac" was a favorite of Sister's and myself. We two never heard a cross word between them. I recall the time I began to tell Mother of a complaint I had about my stepfather and she cut me off. There were two men in her life and they had to get along together; she would listen to no complaint from either one of us! That settled that.

Mr. Mac became a meat cutter and ran the market until we lost it; later he managed a meat market in other grocery stores and/or farmed the land the Cliftons and Mother inherited from Grandpa McCoy.

By graduation in 1921 the recession was apparent and I

was seventeen, and rather immature to enter the University of Alabama. So Mother decided, and it was fine with me, that I should delay entrance for a year, devoting that time to teaching and earning a little money.

By the way, another Elmore County boy, Austin L. Venable of Santuck, graduated from Elmore County High School in Eclectic about the same time. He had a similar interest in teaching history and we were to be college and graduate school roommates. He became a professor at the University of Alabama and we remained friends until his death in 1985.

9

A Young School Teacher

The reasons I include this period in my boyhood memoirs are that I was still young, and most people today have no idea how different the one- and two-room schools in ancient days were from today's consolidated schools.

Upon graduating from high school, we decided it was Troy State I should attend for a six-week summer session, take courses including one on how to teach, seek a job for a year, and then enter the U of A. I had a great time at Troy. I learned of only one vacancy; it was in the Anderson Smith School miles outside Castleberry, and I was lucky enough to get it. One reason was that the vacancy was for a principal of a two-teacher school; in those days that meant a male, and since World War I the veterans didn't seem to apply for such jobs. The other teacher was a woman with several years experience, and I often wondered what she thought of that; of course I never asked.

I took the L.&N.R.R. to Brewton for an orientation session called by the Escambia County Superintendent of Education and then to Castleberry, where I began to realize how informal the life of a school principal could be in those days. I was to be met by a Mr. Monk, who had agreed by mail to give me room and board, but no one met me. At a nearby store I learned that an emergency had prevented Mr. Monk from doing so, but that a friend would pick me up later. He was a farmer with a large family of happy boys, and he drove me in his wagon to his home where I was to spend the night, and a Mr. Albreast would pick me up the next day. This was confusing, but my luck continued.

In Mr. Albreast's buggy the next morning and on the way to *his* home, still further out of Castleberry, I learned that I was to have room and board at the Albreasts' the first semester, because Mr. Monk's parents' home had burned, and they were at the son's for the next three or four months.

What a contrast I would find between the Albreasts' home and the Monks' in the new year. The Albreasts lived on a rural road; to get to the Monks one turned off the road to a lane some miles away that led to the Monks' yard, the very end of the line. I would ask the son of the Monks what lay beyond their land and he replied "Nothing." When pushed, he did add, "Swamps."

The three Albreasts had a pleasant six-room painted house; the four Monks had only two rooms and a lean-to for kitchen and dining rooms. All four Monks would occupy one room and I the other, but mine was unfinished; the place where my fireplace and chimney were to be some day was boarded up sort of. But the climate was warmer that far south in Alabama.

The Albreasts lived one mile from the school; the Monks were two miles away without one structure to be seen on the forest trail to the school. At the Albreasts', we had an excellent variety of meals; at the Monks', the staples would be home-grown rutabagas and collards or turnip greens, but I happened to like these as long as they were all cooked with salt pork, of course. At both meals we had corn bread, biscuits, milk, butter, and molasses. And at both I enjoyed equal kindness and consideration.

My salary was seventy-five dollars a month for seven months, and room and board was fifteen dollars. Who else could ever say, "I was saving four-fifths of my salary?" There was no place to spend money except when we drove in a wagon the long miles to Castleberry on Saturday afternoons, where I could splurge on a Coke and a five-cent pack of peanut butter crackers.

I learned that on the day school opened parents and students would turn up with brush brooms to sweep the school ground and brooms and mops to clean the interior. Then I'd be on my own. I was somewhat like a football player who was very nervous and scared until the first contact. This time that feeling passed when I saw the parents and students were already at work when I arrived on foot at school.

When the yard and rooms were clean, I called the parents and the students to order. There were no song books, so I suggested that we all sing "My Country 'Tis of Thee." This we did for one verse. No one could remember the second verse. But no matter. Other opening services followed and school was in session.

The woman teacher went into the other room with her first three grades. It's strange, but I recall almost nothing about her. I had the fifth, sixth, and seventh grades with a total of twenty-eight students. Happily, there were no fourth graders. A large pot-bellied stove stood in each room. I learned to send a couple of the more reliable students out into the woods to bring back armloads of pine knots which had lots of resin. These turned out to be easily ignited and first-rate fuel.

I tried hard to get to all the subjects each day—there were six at least, if not seven, in each grade. Instead of having each student proceeding at "his or her own pace," I attempted a teaching plan of having each of the three grades studying at *its* own pace. For example, arithmetic assignments were made for each grade and then I would quick-glance at how each student was doing; if necessary, I would sit with a student at his or her desk and make suggestions.

One day I happened to look towards the door and saw a strange man sitting at a desk near the door. I whispered a question to the youngster with whom I was sitting, asking how long the man had been sitting there and learned it had been twenty or thirty minutes. So I walked over and introduced myself, and he turned out to be the superintendent of the Conecuh County schools.

The Smith school was near the Escambia-Conecuh County line, so students of both counties attended. But most of the students resided in Escambia, and that county footed most of the cost of the school; that's why it was Escambia County which had hired me. The visitor suggested that I carry on and at recess we could talk. We did, and he must have liked what he saw, because he said if ever I wanted to change to a Conecuh job to let him know.

I suppose that I should have been pleased, but somehow I thought perhaps he should not proselytize unless of course he first told the superintendent of the Escambia County schools of his intention. This was the first time I was "observed" by an administrator, and it was painless—another piece of pure luck for me.

One student was tall and heavy enough to slaughter me if he tried, and he had a discipline problem. Finally, I picked out a book which had little value if its binding should be broken, and when he next needed reprimanding, I threw the book as hard as I could but I made certain that it was well above his head; it made quite a *splat* when it hit the blackboard. Then I reprimanded him one last time. I don't recommend this act, but I was desperate, and it worked in this case.

We had a basketball court in the schoolyard, so I coached

a boys' team which played a rival a few times. For a couple of games at night we lighted the court by bonfires.

At the end of school we put on a night program in which the students performed for parents and public. Various talents were displayed: recitations of poems, written papers were read, and so on. An unknown man had looked me up and asked if I wanted him at the program as he often had been in the past. Mystified, I asked what he did. So help me, he turned out to be "a fool." That is, he played the fool or jester-clown such as had been done centuries earlier by noblemen and princes.

Learning that the students and parents would not be upset at his clowning as each student performed—indeed many would expect it—I agreed. And he acted up, but he could never have gone over as a professional jester.

I attended another old-time practice in the community in which men sat around in the evening and vied with one another to see who could think of the biggest lie to tell. Also I attended a nighttime taffy candy pull, a favorite practice by youths.

So the school year came to a close in early April in time for the students to get into the strawberry fields. The going rate was two cents for each box of berries picked, and these were placed in crates. When enough crates were collected in Castleberry to fill a box car chilled by blocks of ice, they were shipped to a large northern hub and then would be directed by telegraph to the city which at the moment offered the best market.

Each farmer reccived his apportioned share less ten cents a crate. This was the cash crop for small farmers such as the Monks, who certainly did lead a hard life in the berry country.

I must add that when the first teacher in the other room resigned, her replacement turned out to be a young, cute, stub-nosed blonde. I have no trouble remembering her. But a principal had to be careful about his women teachers—fraternizing was out! So the night that school ended we had our first date. And I would soon have my first girlfriend! It happened that she was enrolling in the U. of A. that summer.

To anticipate a bit, we had a date each night for the six weeks summer session at Alabama, but dates on weeknights had to end by 8 or 8:30. On Saturday afternoons we strolled all the way across Tuscaloosa, practicing the new fad of holding hands while walking, and had a swim. Then we walked back to a hot dog stand for supper. She would have one hamburger, I had two, and we each had a tall Orange Crush. Perhaps we did have an apple or peach tart. The total cost was thirty or thirty-five cents.

Afterwards, we sought the unoccupied steps of some university building. On Saturday nights dates could last until ten p.m. I recall that I had one A, one B, one C that half of summer school. Sadly, she then went home to Eutaw, but I got three A's the second half. As so often happens, she and I slowly drifted apart.

Thereafter, I was in Wetumpka on longer college holidays only, there being none of the current practice of going home for weekends. On the U. of A. campus in regular session, I knew of only one student who had a car, and he was a married man with children. Other students arrived by train with a large trunk.

At that time admission was easy: a diploma from a standard high school and a five dollar fee. However, the grades came out each half-semester, and when we saw drays at the backs of dormitories, they were there to pick up the trunks of students who had been suspended for academic reasons. The passing grade for juniors and seniors was "C."

So now my boyhood days were over. The university treated us as grown-ups, except for dating. We liked that, but now I realize I would have profited from more advice or counselling: I needed more advice on the best courses in which to enroll for a future career as a college professor.

I did get advice on requirements for a teaching certificate, since I knew I would need one to teach in high school for a few years at least. I could also save money for graduate school.

10

Conclusion

I am so pleased to add that I had just the type of career for which I had hoped: a Ph.D. and forty-four happy years teaching in such places as LaFayette, Alabama, High, the U. of Alabama (one year and many summers which meant I could see Mother more than usual), Temple U., and thirty-four years at the U. of Rhode Island.

I must confess I did have one job in which I was miserable. It was in a high school in which the administration and teachers had a very different policy and practice from my own. If the students did not do well in early tests (in other words, if they were drones), I gave lower marks, even a large number of F's, knowing that they could and would work harder and soon make higher grades.

Without waiting for the latter, I got the reputation of being out of line and because I "couldn't pass as many" was probably a poor teacher. But once again the Guardian Angels came to my rescue as they had when I got the Anderson Little job near Castleberry: out of a clear blue sky, I had a phone call with an offer from Marion Institute, to which I had also applied for a job.

I expressed appreciation, but with the saddest heart answered that I could not just walk out from the job I had accepted. (The call was from Tubby Williams.) Wanting to boast a bit I reported the offer and rejection to the administrators. I knew they were not pleased with me, but I was not prepared for them to volunteer an offer to release me within two weeks. I rushed back to the phone, got that job, and the year was saved after all.

Also, besides publishing a score of articles of a scholarly nature on history and archives, I was the author of two volumes, and the first editor of two others, all four of which were well-received by reviewers.

Until each was broken by the same incurable disease, I had the best of good fortunes in my two marriages. But I do have a daughter—need I add that her name is Margaret Ann—and she is not yet forty years old. She lives nearby and gives me much pleasure by her good company in my late years.

My mother lived until her ninety-seventh year. Among our most enjoyable were her last seven years when I had retired and could spend months with her. I recall one evening when she remarked once again: "We seem to have such a short time together." So I had her add up with me the various lengths of time we had spent together that very day, and it came to seven-and-a-half hours.

She replied, "True, but it didn't seem that long."

www.ingramcontent.com/pod-product-compliance
Lightning Source LLC
Chambersburg PA
CBHW031656040426
42453CB00006B/327